j921

Purdie.
nature's laws :
ut Isaac Newton

A Creative Minds Biography

DISCOVERING NATURE'S LAWS

A Story about Isaac Newton

by Laura Purdie Salas

illustrations by Emily C. S. Reynolds

Carolrhoda Books, Inc./Minneapolis

For my two daughters, who remind me of Isaac: Maddy, who thinks deeply and creatively about the meaning of the universe, and Annabelle, who brings passion and determination to all her pursuits —L. P. S.

For Matthew, the miracle in my life, and for my mom and dad, whose example of learning is never-ending —E. C. S. R.

The author wishes to thank Scott Mandelbrote, Official Fellow and Director of Studies in History, University of Cambridge, for his help in answering questions and for reading this manuscript for accuracy.

Text copyright © 2004 by Laura Purdie Salas
Illustrations copyright © 2004 by Emily C. S. Reynolds

This book is available in two editions:
Library binding by Carolrhoda Books, Inc.,
  a division of Lerner Publishing Group
Soft cover by First Avenue Editions,
  an imprint of Lerner Publishing Group
241 First Avenue North
Minneapolis, MN 55401 U.S.A.

Website address: www.lernerbooks.com

Library of Congress Cataloging-in-Publication Data

Salas, Laura Purdie.
    Discovering nature's laws : a story about Isaac Newton / by Laura
Purdie Salas ; illustrations by Emily C. S. Reynolds.
        p.   cm. — (A creative minds biography)
    Includes bibliographical references and index.
    Summary: A biography of physicist Sir Isaac Newton, who invented
calculus, discovered a law of gravity, and made other significant scientific
discoveries in the seventeenth and eighteenth centuries.
    ISBN: 1–57505–183–4 (lib. bdg. : alk. paper)
    ISBN: 1–57505–606–2 (pbk. : alk. paper)
    1. Newton, Isaac, Sir, 1642–1727—Juvenile literature. 2. Physicists—
Great Britain—Biography—Juvenile literature. [1. Newton, Isaac, Sir,
1642–1727. 2. Physicists. 3. Scientists.] I. Reynolds, Emily C. S., ill.
II. Title. III. Series.
QC16.N7S25 2004
530'.092—dc21   2003005583

Manufactured in the United States of America
1 2 3 4 5 6 – JR – 09 08 07 06 05 04

Table of Contents

Fire in the Sky   5

Not Fit for Farming   13

The Miracle Years   23

Success and Arguments   33

The Principia   43

Newton at the Mint   51

Newton's Major Discoveries   60

Bibliography   61

Index   63

1

Fire in the Sky

Twelve-year-old Isaac Newton had an idea. One night in 1655, he lit his paper lantern and attached it to a kite. He stood in an open, windy field and sailed the kite into the dark English sky.

The flame danced and flickered in the air. It terrified the people of Grantham. In the 1650s, people in England were not used to seeing moving lights in the sky.

When market day came, all the townspeople were talking about the mysterious light. Nobody guessed that Isaac had anything to do with it. Many people thought the flashing light was a comet. But it was just another of Isaac Newton's bright ideas.

═══

In October 1642, before Isaac was born, his father died. Two months later, on Christmas Day, Isaac was born at Woolsthorpe Manor, his family's estate.

5

He was so tiny he could have fit into a one-quart milk jug. Nobody thought Isaac would survive. When two women walked to a neighbor's house for his medicine, they stopped to sit on a fence and chat. They were so sure he would die that they didn't hurry.

Isaac did survive. Still, there was little celebration at Woolsthorpe. Isaac's mother, Hannah Ayscough, was still grieving over the death of Isaac's father.

When Isaac was three years old, Hannah married Barnabas Smith, an older minister in a nearby village. Her new husband refused to raise someone else's child. So Hannah went to live with her husband and left Isaac behind.

Hannah's parents came to stay at Woolsthorpe. They raised Isaac and ran the estate with the help of the servants. Even though Hannah and her new husband lived only a mile away, Isaac rarely saw his mother and her new family.

Isaac lived in an attic bedroom at Woolsthorpe. All alone, he drew pictures on his walls. He drew birds, animals, people, ships, and plants. He even carved pictures into the windowsill. But he had no friends to play with. And he did not feel close to his grandparents. Since his father had died, his stepfather didn't want him, and his mother had abandoned him, he probably wondered when they would disappear, too.

When Isaac was ten years old, Barnabas Smith died. Hannah came home to Woolsthorpe with her three new children. Suddenly, Isaac's lonely life was turned inside out by a mother and half siblings he hardly knew. There was four-year-old Mary, two-year-old Benjamin, and baby Hannah.

But that life didn't last long. When Isaac was eleven years old, his mother sent him to King's School in Grantham. The school was seven miles away. It was too far to travel by horse every day. So Isaac stayed with Mr. Clark, the town druggist. The headmaster placed Isaac in the lowest class with younger children. Isaac was shy and unsociable. He did not make good grades, and he didn't make good friends, either.

Isaac struggled at Mr. Clark's house, as well. Mr. Clark taught Isaac about chemistry. He taught him how to gather herbs for medicines. But Isaac had no patience and often became irritated with Mr. Clark.

Mr. Clark had two stepsons, Arthur and Edward, and a stepdaughter called Miss Storer, who was a few years younger than Isaac. Isaac did not get along with Arthur and Edward. He stole from Edward and fought with Arthur. But he did enjoy spending time with Miss Storer. He liked to build doll tables and cupboards for her. The fact that Isaac preferred to play with girls made him even more of an outcast.

One morning when Isaac was walking to school, Arthur Storer kicked him in the stomach. Isaac was filled with rage and challenged Arthur to a fight. After school, the two boys fought in the churchyard. The schoolmaster's son egged them on by clapping one on the back and winking at the other. He wanted to see a good fight. Eleven-year-old Isaac was smaller than Arthur and not very athletic, but he was out of control. He pounded Arthur.

Isaac decided that beating Arthur up wasn't enough. He wanted to beat him academically, too. So Isaac threw himself into his studies. Soon he was a top student.

Isaac began a fitful habit of studying. He worked intensely on his studies for a few weeks or months. Then he turned his attention to something else and ignored his schoolwork. Gadgets or model building often captured his attention. But when another student got better grades than he did, he abandoned his models and began studying again. His wild mood swings, problems getting along with other people, and intense enthusiasms may have been caused by bipolar syndrome.

As a teenager, Isaac tried to use his intelligence to become popular. He performed tricks like the flying lantern, but other boys were suspicious of him. They found Isaac completely strange.

Even though it didn't help win him friends, Isaac continued to build gadgets. He especially liked making sundials. Most villages used sundials to tell time. The sun cast a shadow over the pin of the sundial. The shadow fell along a circle of marks, and people checked the position of that shadow to learn the time. Sundials could be as small as a coin or bigger than a football field.

Isaac built sundials in almost every room of Mr. Clark's house. He put pegs right into the walls to show hours. He tied strings along the walls to mark the sun's shadow on different days. Isaac even invented a ceiling sundial.

Isaac used sundials for more than just telling time. He used them to tell what day of the month it was. He figured out when the sun would pass the equator. He knew when the longest and shortest days of the year would be. The discovery that he could predict what happened in nature with a machine gave Isaac a new sense of power.

He had a gift for understanding the way mechanical gadgets worked. Once, a new windmill was being built outside town. People gathered to watch the construction. Isaac carefully examined the windmill. When he got home, he made a small model of it. He made cloth sails and set it up on the roof.

Then Isaac decided to use mouse power instead of wind power. He built a little treadmill inside his mill. He found a mouse to run on it. A farmer gave Isaac corn to tempt the mouse into running. If that didn't work, Isaac would tug on a small string tied to the mouse's tail. Neighbors visited to see the "mouse miller." Isaac's models and inventions amused the people of Grantham.

When he was about sixteen, Isaac and Miss Storer grew even closer. He continued to make her gifts and enjoyed showing off his skill with tools. She believed Isaac was in love with her and that they would marry. Isaac spent a lot of time with her, but he did not ask her to marry him. He kept his feelings, whether they were friendship or love, to himself.

When Isaac was seventeen, his mother called him home. She wanted Isaac to learn to run the family farm. Isaac Newton, the strange genius who built wonderful models and inventions, was going to be a farmer. It was time for him to live an ordinary life.

2

Not Fit for Farming

Hannah thought her clever son would quickly learn the business of farming. So she assigned a dependable servant to teach Isaac how to care for the animals and buy supplies.

But Isaac did not learn quickly. He built gadgets when he was supposed to watch the animals. He didn't notice when the sheep or pigs wandered off. Neighbors complained when the animals got into their crops.

Market days in Grantham bored Isaac. He often bribed the servant to let him out of the carriage just around the corner from Woolsthorpe. He would then spend the entire day building gadgets in the field. Meanwhile, the servant sold the farm's produce.

Sometimes Isaac did go into town. But he still did not help out at the market. Instead, he spent the day at Mr. Clark's house. He liked reading Mr. Clark's books about philosophy—what people called physical science at that time—as well as botany, anatomy, and math. At home, Isaac treated people poorly. He punched his sisters and fought with the servants. He called people names. Isaac seemed happiest spending time alone. Games, farming, and friendship did not interest him. He just wanted to be left alone with his books and his tools.

Hannah's brother was a clergyman. In England in the 1600s, the clergy were the most educated people. They had the time and the background to study philosophy. Hannah's brother thought Isaac should finish school and enter the university. The headmaster at King's School in Grantham also wanted Isaac to return. But Isaac's mother wanted him to run the farm. So the servant continued to work with him.

Isaac continued his absentminded ways. Sometimes he even forgot to eat. The servant was amazed. If a man couldn't remember to feed his own belly, how on earth would he remember to take care of the animals? The servant gave up on teaching Isaac. Even Isaac's mother began to see that her plan would not work.

The headmaster at King's School offered to pay for Isaac's schooling himself. He said that Isaac could live with him while attending school.

In the autumn of 1660, Hannah finally admitted that Isaac was not a farmer. Isaac returned to King's School in Grantham to prepare for the university. He was eighteen. He had lasted only nine months at Woolsthorpe. The servants were glad to see Isaac go. They thought Isaac was lazy and had no common sense. They liked to say that he was "fit for nothing but the 'Versity."

Isaac finished his studies at King's School in nine months. In June of 1661, he traveled three days to Cambridge University. He bought a desk lock, ink for his pen, a notebook, candles, and a chamber pot. Isaac entered Trinity College, the most well-known college at Cambridge.

Isaac's mother could easily afford to pay for his schooling, but she refused. So Isaac entered Trinity College as a subsizar, earning his schooling by waiting on other students. He woke them for chapel, brushed their hair, and emptied their chamber pots. The boy who was used to having servants had become one.

Wealthier students looked down upon the subsizars. As usual, Isaac had trouble getting along with the other students. He spent much of his time alone, wandering the rainy, damp grounds of Cambridge.

Isaac was relieved to continue his education, but he soon found that Cambridge University was behind the times. The Scientific Revolution was sweeping across Europe. Scientists were observing the natural world. They were performing experiments to test theories and answer questions. Instead of just accepting that the sun rose in the east, scientists were showing mathematically how it happened. They were accumulating facts, asking questions, and performing experiments. But not at Cambridge University, which was more than four hundred years old and kept to its traditions.

Cambridge professors still focused on the teachings of Aristotle, a Greek philosopher who had lived two thousand years earlier. Aristotle had believed that nature was orderly. He had said that logic must be used in every branch of science. He felt science must follow basic laws, but he did not think of using math and experiments to try to define those laws. The equipment available during Aristotle's lifetime was limited. He had no microscope and no telescope.

But in the past one hundred years, scientists had

started to shatter accepted truths. For example, scientists had long believed that heavier items would drop faster than lighter items. About seventy years earlier, Galileo Galilei proved that was not true. He based his study on an experiment where a scientist had dropped different items off the Leaning Tower of Pisa.

Most Cambridge students were totally unaware of recent scientific discoveries. They were simply ambitious men who wanted to become educated. Most wanted the safe career of a minister. They were willing to accept Aristotle's views without question, even though the Scientific Revolution was quickly passing them by.

Isaac's tutor, Benjamin Pulleyn, introduced him to the standard books. Isaac found all of the texts too easy. He never finished reading most of them. "Plato and Aristotle are my friends," he wrote. "But my best friend is Truth." Isaac didn't want to be told how the world worked. He wanted to prove it for himself. He wanted to find his own way to the truth.

The students and teachers at Cambridge were out of date. But Cambridge had one crucial thing for Isaac: books. Isaac found books in the library on history, the stars and planets, and philosophy. He devoured these books, teaching himself complicated subjects.

A book by René Descartes introduced Isaac to the wonders of mathematics. He studied the writings of Nicolaus Copernicus, who said the Sun, not Earth, was the center of the universe. He read the works of Johannes Kepler, who had calculated the positions of the planets. He studied Galileo, who had conducted experiments that disproved several of Aristotle's theories.

Isaac began to form his own vision of the universe. He believed the universe worked according to rules. He felt there was order everywhere and that huge planets and single drops of water all followed the same scientific laws. And he believed that mathematics would reveal those laws.

Isaac's search for knowledge took almost all of his attention. In the summer of 1662, however, Isaac suddenly experienced intense religious feelings. He drew up a list of sins from his past. It included the way he had treated his family and the servants. He wrote his list in code, so that nobody else could read it.

Isaac realized he did not believe in the Trinity of the Father, Son, and Holy Spirit. He believed that Jesus was the son of God, but he didn't believe that Jesus was equal to God. But Isaac kept his religious beliefs to himself. Belief in the Trinity was central to the Church of England, and Cambridge University was closely tied to the Church of England. Isaac would not be allowed to attend Trinity College if he revealed his true beliefs.

Soon Isaac stopped writing about religion and focused on math and science again. As Isaac read, he jotted down questions. He came up with ideas for experiments and then performed them. Once, he looked directly at the sun and almost blinded himself. Another time, he slipped a blunt needle into his eye socket to change the curve of his retina. His determined search for the truth led him to do reckless things.

By 1664 mathematics consumed all of Isaac's time. He taught himself all of the current mathematical theories in just one year. Isaac learned it all from his beloved books.

That year, Isaac earned a scholarship. His mathematics professor, Isaac Barrow, helped him. Professor Barrow was popular, witty, and outgoing—the complete opposite of Isaac. But he admired Isaac's abilities more than Isaac's own tutor did. This scholarship allowed Isaac to study at Cambridge for four more years, and he didn't have to be a subsizar anymore.

Isaac studied like a desperate man. He could not be bothered with silly things like eating and sleeping. He forgot his meals, and his cat grew plump on dinners of Isaac's gruel and eggs with milk.

Sometimes, Isaac stayed awake all night. He studied by candlelight, or he watched the night sky. He loved to gaze at comets, stars, and planets.

Isaac was extremely independent. He studied what he wanted to, totally ignoring Cambridge University's requirements. One Sunday, Isaac went to a town fair. A sparkling prism caught his eye, and he bought it. Isaac began to experiment with the prism that very day.

Despite Isaac's refusal to follow the standard course of study, he earned his bachelor of arts degree in the summer of 1665. He loved the books, the ideas, and the solitude of academic life. More than anything, he wanted to stay at Cambridge and continue studying.

3

The Miracle Years

In the summer of 1665, the plague broke out in England. Fleas on rats spread the vicious disease. People infected by the fleas got headaches, fevers, and swollen armpits and necks. Most died in agony within days.

Thirty-one thousand people died of the plague in London that summer. Body collectors pushed carts through the streets. "Bring out your dead!" they yelled. Some weeks, more than two thousand people died. Everyone who could afford to leave the city did. In the country, there were fewer rats and fleas.

Isaac left Trinity College. He headed home on horseback to Woolsthorpe. Soon the entire college closed down. The students were instructed to go to the countryside.

While the plague spread throughout European cities, Isaac continued his studies alone. At twenty-two years old, he knew more math than any other person alive. Neither books nor tutors could teach him anymore.

In 1665 Isaac developed a new kind of math called calculus. Among its many uses, calculus dealt with objects in motion. Isaac knew that if a man walked five miles down a straight road at a constant speed, it was simple to calculate where that man would be at any given time. But what if the man sped up and slowed down? What if the road curved?

Calculus let Isaac solve problems involving accelerating objects. He proved Johannes Kepler's belief that the planets traveled around the Sun in an elliptical, or oval, orbit rather than a circle. But Isaac was secretive and afraid of being criticized. He didn't tell anybody of his new math.

During that year, Isaac gave up trying to be like other people. He finally accepted that the pursuit of knowledge was his life's passion. He became comfortable with the idea that he would study and live a solitary life.

After he developed calculus, Isaac lost interest in it. He could have tried to use the new method to answer more questions. Instead, he moved on to study theories of force and impact, an area of science called mechanics.

René Descartes had said that an object would continue in its same state unless an outside force acted on it. For example, a ball lying still would continue to lie still until something hit it.

Isaac built upon Descartes's ideas. He said that the mass and speed of the force would determine its impact on the object. A cow kicking a ball would have more impact than a feather blowing against the same ball. Isaac had made an important insight into mechanics. Even so, he did not pursue this idea further.

One particular question fascinated Isaac. Why didn't the Moon shoot off into space? He knew that a body in circular motion tried to move away from the center. For example, a stone whirled around on a string swung out as far as the string would reach. But there was no string holding the Moon to Earth. So, what kept the Moon from spinning away?

One day in 1666, Isaac sat in the Woolsthorpe garden thinking about that question. An apple fell to the ground. Isaac wondered several things. Why does the apple always fall straight to the ground? Why does it never go upward or sideways? Why does it always fall toward Earth's center? Does the force called gravity pull the apple toward Earth's center? Could gravity hold the Moon in place, too?

Isaac wanted to prove that gravity held the Moon in orbit. Other mathematicians had developed the math to calculate the force needed to keep an object moving in a circular orbit. But planets had elliptical orbits, as Kepler had described in 1609. So Isaac developed a way to determine the force needed for an elliptical orbit.

The Sun's gravity pulled all planets, Isaac said. But it did not affect all planets equally. He figured that if the Sun pulled on planet A with a certain amount of gravity, then the Sun pulled on a planet twice as far away as planet A with only ¼ of the force. And it pulled on a planet three times as far away as planet A with only ⅑ of the force. Isaac had determined that gravity followed what was called an inverse square law.

Isaac discovered this inverse square law of gravity by "thinking on it continually," he said. Again, he did not tell anyone about his discovery. He did not seek fame or fortune, only truth. Once he understood the truth of gravity, he moved on to another subject.

He dove into the study of light and color. Scientist Robert Hooke believed that light was made of waves. In a book published in 1665, he wrote that the waves for each color of light had different strengths and rhythms. Isaac disagreed with Hooke. He began experimenting to discover the nature of light.

First, he closed the shutters in his room. Then he poked a small round hole in the shutters to let the sun through. Next, he placed a prism between the shutters and the opposite wall, twenty-two feet away. As sunlight passed through the prism, a spectrum of all the colors of the rainbow appeared on the opposite wall. Isaac noticed that the colors made an oblong shape on the wall. He wondered why that happened. Isaac decided that it must be because the prism bent the different colors at different angles. He wrote, "It was at first a very pleasing divertissement, to view the vivid and intense colours produced thereby." He enjoyed thinking about things. But performing experiments was his favorite part of figuring out the world.

Many scientists believed that a prism changed light. They thought it darkened white light into other colors. But Isaac said the prism simply revealed the true nature of sunlight.

He used another experiment to prove this. He let light shine through two prisms. If prisms changed light, the colors should get even darker when they went through the second prism. But the colors stayed the same. Isaac was right. The prism only separated out the parts of light. It did not change them.

Isaac also wanted to prove that white light was made up of all other colors. He cast three overlapping spectrums on the wall. The overlapping colors combined to make white. So white light was a combination of all the other colors of the spectrum.

The plague continued to lay waste to London. Then on September 1, 1666, the Great Fire of London started. The four-day blaze destroyed 87 churches and more than 13,000 homes. But it also killed many of London's rats, so the plague was slowed down.

Isaac kept studying and experimenting. He scribbled page after page with his feather pen. He changed his handwriting to make it faster. He even found new ways to make ink, probably because he used so much of it. He knew he was making amazing advances in the topics he studied. He said he was "in the prime of my age for . . . Mathematicks & Philosophy."

Nobody in Europe knew as much math as twenty-three-year-old Isaac. And only one other man knew as much science as he did. That was Dutch scientist

Christiaan Huygens. Huygens was the inventor of the pendulum clock. It was more accurate than earlier clocks and could be used after dark, when sundials were useless. He was the leader of the Royal Academy of Science in Paris. He was also an honorary member of the Royal Society in London. This small group of scientists had been founded by King Charles II in 1662. Huygens regularly wrote to them about his latest discoveries.

Scientists all over Europe often wrote back and forth to each other. Papers were read at meetings of scientific societies, and then other scientists would comment on the papers. Sometimes scientists' papers were officially published by the Royal Society or by other publishers of scientific material. Then copies would be printed and anybody who wished could buy a copy.

Isaac knew of Huygens's research and agreed with parts of it. He used some of Huygens's formulas to help him with his own studies. But Isaac felt he could prove some of Huygens's work wrong. He chose not to show anyone his papers or try to get them published. Isaac still worked alone, unknown.

The two years Isaac spent at Woolsthorpe during the plague were his "miracle years." His studies laid the groundwork for later advances in gravity, mechanics, and optics, the study of light. Amazingly, he made these advances by himself, with no formal study and no teacher.

While Isaac was at Woolsthorpe during the plague, he occasionally saw his old friend Miss Storer. But Isaac did nothing to further their relationship. Miss Storer finally realized that she could not compete with Isaac's fascination for the laws of nature. She gave up hope of marrying Isaac.

4

Success and Arguments

Isaac Newton returned to Cambridge in April 1667. Nobody knew about his amazing studies. He acted like the same old absentminded Isaac. He wore dirty clothes and forgot to comb his long hair. He sat down to his dinner. But then he began to scribble on scraps of paper and forgot to eat.

Newton earned his master's degree. Then he returned to his study of colors and optics. He wrote a paper called "De Analysi" about infinite series of numbers. Professor Barrow was impressed by the paper. He passed it along to many leading mathematicians. But Newton would not let anyone publish it. Newton still did not have friends, but the students and professors began to recognize his intelligence.

In 1669 Professor Barrow retired. Barrow was the most advanced mathematician at Cambridge. He recognized Newton's genius and nominated Newton to replace him. Newton accepted the job. He became the youngest math professor ever to teach at Cambridge.

Newton was not a talented speaker. His lectures were far too advanced for his students. Often, nobody showed up, and Newton lectured to an empty room.

Newton began to study telescopes. The telescopes of the 1600s magnified objects by passing light through a curved lens. The lens bent the light and converged it on one point, producing an image. But light entering the thinner lens edges did not reach the same point of focus as light entering the thicker lens center. Because of this, the light and image never met up perfectly. With lenses, telescopes didn't achieve exact focus. Stars studied with these telescopes often appeared to be surrounded by fuzzy rainbow halos.

Newton built a telescope that focused light with a mirror instead of a lens. A precisely made, curved mirror reflected each color to the same point of focus. Perfect focus could be obtained, so the colorful halos disappeared.

Newton curved the mirrors and made all the parts himself. He took great pride in building the entire telescope from scratch. His six-inch-long telescope made objects appear about forty times closer than they actually were.

News of the telescope set the Royal Society of London buzzing. The society asked Newton to send a model of it. Isaac Barrow, who kept in touch with Newton, took the telescope to London. He showed it to King Charles II and the Royal Society.

The scientists were impressed. They invited Newton to join their group.

Newton's first attempt at sharing his ideas had gone rather well. He enjoyed the attention that his telescope received. He made friends with astronomer Edmund Halley and medical doctor and philosopher John Locke. He even began to feel like part of the scientific community.

In 1672 he went one step further. He sent Henry Oldenburg of the Royal Society a paper about colors and light. Oldenburg read Newton's work to the society, and the society published the paper. Newton's writings were made public for the first time. Most members were impressed with Newton's work. Once again, he enjoyed their approval.

Robert Hooke, however, sent Newton a long letter

criticizing his paper. Newton replied angrily. This debate of ideas was common for scientists, but Newton took the disagreement personally.

Newton wanted recognition for his work, but he could not handle the criticism. He swore that he would never publish anything again.

Newton's focus shifted to alchemy in the 1670s. Alchemy was the search for something called the philosopher's stone, a substance that could change metals into gold. Newton, though, was not concerned with gold. Legend also said that the philosopher's stone would perfect anything it touched. If a human tasted it, that person would be cured of any sicknesses. The person might even live forever.

Newton thought the philosopher's stone would reveal the true nature of life and how God worked in the world. Newton studied alchemy books and performed hundreds of experiments. He kept his fascination secret, though. Most scientists thought that alchemy was a complete waste of time.

In 1675 Newton heard some disturbing news. A German scholar named Gottfried Leibniz claimed that he could solve math problems involving slopes and curved lines. Newton had developed calculus during the plague years, and calculus would solve these sorts of problems. But Newton had not shown anyone his calculations. Nobody knew that Newton had also figured out how to solve these problems.

Leibniz's claim bothered Newton, but he still kept his methods secret. He wrote several sentences explaining his method. Then he used a special code to describe the sentences. He figured that this would prove he knew the methods now if he later revealed the code and the sentences. But his calculus innovations were twelve years old. And Leibniz had already gone public.

Leibniz did not want to play games. He showed his methods to the Royal Society in the summer of 1677. That put an end to the dispute. Newton and Leibniz each felt that he alone had developed the methods and that the matter was closed.

Newton faced another problem. At Cambridge, every new professor had to become a clergyman for the Church of England within seven years. Newton had no interest in becoming a clergyman. He just wanted to be left alone to think, study, and experiment. Besides, he did not believe all the teachings of the Church of England.

Once again, Isaac Barrow helped him out. He went to see King Charles II, and he convinced the king to excuse Newton from becoming a clergyman. As long as Newton did not commit a crime, disagree publicly with the Church of England, or get married, he would be allowed to stay at Cambridge University indefinitely. Newton could continue to keep his religious beliefs secret.

In 1679 Hooke and Newton exchanged some letters about orbits and gravity. In one of his letters, Hooke mentioned the inverse square law of gravity. It was a law that Newton had discovered during the miracle years at Woolsthorpe. Since then, Huygens had discovered the inverse square law of gravity, too. He had published his findings. Since Newton had kept his discovery to himself, nobody knew he had been the first to discover this law of gravity.

The same year, Newton's half brother Benjamin came down with a fever. Their mother, Hannah, nursed Benjamin to health, but she caught his fever. Although Newton had only visited Woolsthorpe a few times since the plague years, he went home to Woolsthorpe to care for his mother. He sat up through the nights with her, bandaging her blisters.

Despite Newton's efforts, his mother died. Newton returned to Cambridge and threw himself back into his studies. He focused intensely on math. He lived mostly on bread and water. He took naps fully dressed. His secretary, a boy named Humphrey, said he only saw Newton laugh one time in five years.

In the summer of 1684, Edmund Halley came to visit. The astronomer wanted Newton to answer a question neither Halley nor Hooke could answer. Would the inverse square law of gravity work on elliptical orbits? Newton assured him that it did. He had proved this when he was at Woolsthorpe studying gravity in 1666. But then he told Halley that he couldn't find his proof of it. As soon as Halley left, Newton dove back into his studies of gravity. That fall, he lectured on gravity and the planets at Cambridge.

In November, Newton sent a paper to Halley. It contained a mathematical explanation of why the planets have elliptical orbits around the Sun. Halley was amazed. He convinced Newton to publish a book on the subject.

Newton planned a book of three parts. He wanted to do much more than just prove the inverse square law of gravity worked for elliptical orbits. Until this time, Newton had worked on his studies intensely but erratically. He had not worked for publication. He had not worked for fame. The only reward he sought was truth. Finally, Newton was writing a book to share his discoveries. He would show the world what he could do.

For nearly two years, Newton concentrated on his book. He completed a draft of Book 1 in the spring of 1686. That April, his manuscript was presented to the Royal Society.

When Hooke saw the manuscript, he said that Newton should give him credit for suggesting the inverse square law of gravity. Newton was furious. He had developed and proved the law himself. But after some arguing, he agreed to include a statement in future drafts giving Hooke some credit for the idea.

Then the Royal Society decided it could not afford to publish the book. So Halley offered to finance the publication himself. Halley did not have a lot of extra money. But he felt strongly that Newton's book must be published.

Then Newton decided not to publish it. He feared criticism and controversy. He decided he would not share his findings with the world after all.

5

The Principia

Edmund Halley really wanted Newton to publish his book. He knew Newton's work was too important to keep secret. He finally talked Newton into letting him publish it. *Philosophiae Naturalis Principia Mathematica,* or *Mathematical Principles of Natural Philosophy,* was printed in the summer of 1687. Newton was forty-four years old. *The Principia,* as it was called, contained three books. In the preface to Book 1, Newton explained his three laws of motion:

1. *Law of inertia:* A body in motion tends to remain in motion and a body at rest tends to remain at rest unless it is acted on by an outside force.

That explained why, if Newton were riding a galloping horse that suddenly stopped, he would likely fly right over the front of the horse. His body would remain in motion even after the horse stopped.

2. *Law of acceleration:* The acceleration of an object depends on the object's mass and the force applied to it.

If Newton pushed a cannonball, he would probably not send the ball very far or fast in any direction. But if Newton pushed an orange, the orange's smaller mass would allow it to roll farther and faster.

3. *Law of action and reaction:* For every action, there is an equal and opposite reaction.

If Newton rowed a boat across a lake, his oars would push some water toward the back of the boat. Each time he pushed the water backward, the boat would move forward.

Book 1 discussed Newton's law of universal gravitation. That law says that every object in the universe is attracted to every other object. Newton showed that the force of each attraction is related to the objects' masses and the distance between their centers.

Book 2 described Newton's experiments.

Book 3 showed how his ideas could be useful. Newton called this book *The System of the World.* In it, he explained the shape of Earth. He also showed why Earth's axis changed direction over the centuries and why comets traveled in elliptical orbits.

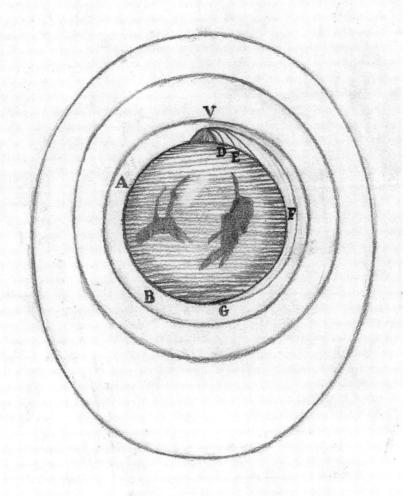

Illustration from The Principia: *Newton's theory of how a cannonball could go into orbit.*

The Principia showed that nature was not just some random force. Nature followed certain laws of behavior, and Isaac Newton had figured out some of those laws.

Newton received plenty of attention when *The Principia* was published. Mathematicians and scientists throughout Europe read and discussed it, though few understood it.

Until then, most scientists did not believe mathematics could help explain the universe. They had never heard of the ideas in Newton's book. Students at Cambridge joked about their teacher who had written the book nobody understood. But even scientists who could not understand Newton's math began to see the universe as orderly. They began studying mechanics and astronomy with fresh enthusiasm. *The Principia* changed the course of science.

Robert Hooke still claimed that Newton had stolen his ideas of gravity. That law was the centerpiece of Newton's entire work. Newton was outraged. Some people believed Newton, and some people believed Hooke. For months, people debated. Recognizing Newton's brilliance, most members of the Royal Society agreed that Newton certainly should get the credit for discovering that the inverse square law of gravity applied to planets.

Hooke had indeed stated this thought at times, though he had not provided the calculations necessary to prove it. Newton had both made the connection and proved it through painstaking calculations. Finally the controversy died down.

Newton was famous throughout Europe. Not everybody agreed with his ideas, but almost everyone agreed he was a genius. The scientific world watched to see what he would do next.

But Newton had no interest in what the world was waiting for. He became interested in politics. He ran for Parliament in 1689 and won. He spent one year in London. He voted for the Bill of Rights, which limited the power of the king, and the Toleration Act, which allowed more religious freedom.

Secretly, Newton worked on religious papers. Newton wanted to assign dates to events in the Bible. He didn't believe history books or the findings of archaeologists. Newton trusted the skies. If the Bible said an event happened during an eclipse, he would search through old star maps to try to figure out the year of the event.

He also worked on interpreting the Book of Revelation and the mathematical aspects of the Bible. For example, he tried to figure out the exact size of the cubit, the measure Noah used in building the ark.

For more than five years, Newton concentrated on religion and alchemy studies. Many of his alchemy experiments required a blazing fire. A fire once got out of hand and burned up some of his work.

For his experiments, Newton used the symbolism that he learned in alchemy books. Planets represented metals. Lions, dragons, doves, and eagles represented various actions. When Newton figured out a way to vaporize tin, he wrote, "I made Jupiter fly on the wings of the eagle!"

Then in 1693, at the age of fifty, Isaac suffered a severe mental breakdown. He believed his friends were plotting against him or deserting him. He began to argue with them. He wrote to Samuel Pepys, an adviser to the king, "I must withdraw from your acquaintance, and see neither you nor the rest of my friends any more."

Isaac's breakdown might have been caused by a number of things. The fire had upset him terribly. He might have had mercury poisoning from years of chemical experiments. His bipolar disorder might have gotten worse. Or it might have just been long years of too much work and too little sleep.

Newton's severe mental problems lasted for a year or so. As he began feeling better, he apologized to his friends.

Newton wrote to Samuel Pepys that he had not felt well the previous year. He said that before he wrote to him, he had slept "for 5 nights together not a wink." Newton blamed his illness on exhaustion and lack of sleep.

He also wrote to John Locke. He said he had been so upset with Locke that when someone told him that Locke was sick, he answered that it was better if Locke were dead. Newton wrote to Locke, "I desire you to forgive me this uncharitableness."

Locke and Pepys both forgave him.

By 1696 Newton felt healthier. But after more than thirty years at Cambridge, he was ready to leave. Newton had enjoyed London when he was in Parliament. He decided to look for a job in London.

He got a job offer. Did he want to be the warden of the mint, the place where coins were made for England? He did. He was eager to move to London and leave behind his life of intense study. As warden, he would oversee the mint. Within a month, he moved to London.

6

Newton at the Mint

The mint was located between the inner and outer walls of the Tower of London. Horses powered many of the machines at the mint. The whole area smelled horsey. Newton soon bought his own house outside of the Tower. He purchased red drapes and a couch and moved in. Catherine Barton, his niece, moved in to be his hostess and housekeeper.

Usually, the warden enjoyed the pay and prestige of running the mint without actually doing much work. Nobody expected Newton to become involved in the day-to-day operation. But he started his new job with enthusiasm.

Newton tested coins to check their levels of silver or gold. His years of measuring metals in alchemy experiments came in handy. And of course the accounting system was no problem for someone with his math skills. He also investigated counterfeiters.

Still, he did not abandon his studies completely. That first year, a Swiss mathematician sent Newton a math problem concerning speed and curves. Newton received the problem at four o'clock in the afternoon. He sat down to work on it. He finished the problem at four o'clock the next morning. But he didn't tell anyone. He was still keeping secrets.

A few years later, Leibniz solved the problem and bragged about it. The old argument over who had invented calculus started back up.

═══

Newton oversaw the recoinage program. New machine-made coins replaced old handmade coins in the huge project. The recoinage was completed in 1698. In 1700 Newton became master of the mint.

He continued working on alchemy. When Hooke died in 1703, Newton became active in the Royal Society again. It had been sixteen years since he had published *The Principia*. But he was elected president of the society shortly after joining.

The next year, he published a book entitled *Opticks*. It contained all his discoveries on light. *Opticks* was a huge success. But its success only intensified the calculus debate. The Royal Society investigated the calculus argument. Newton was president of the Royal Society, and his good friend Halley was on the investigating committee. So the outcome seemed obvious. Even though both Leibniz and Newton still had supporters, the committee found that Newton had developed calculus first.

Newton still spent a lot of time alone. He still took it personally when anyone questioned his claims. But he gave money to charity and to distant relatives. Polite and sometimes even witty, he became more sociable with his niece Catherine's many friends.

In 1705 Queen Anne knighted Newton. Sir Isaac Newton was the first scientist to ever receive this honor. He was famous throughout England and all of Europe. Although most people could not understand his work, everyone knew that he was a genius.

Newton was still master of the mint. Fame no longer bothered him, and he even made a few more close friends. Two friends were William Stukeley, a young London doctor who was a member of the Royal Society, and John Conduitt, who married Catherine in 1717.

In a complete turnaround from his youth, Newton became concerned about his image. He gained weight, wore a wig, and dressed nicely. He had many portraits painted of himself.

In January 1725, Newton caught a bad cough. Catherine thought the pollution in London was responsible. She persuaded him to move out to the country. Newton moved to Kensington, but he remained master of the mint and president of the Royal Society. On March 2, 1727, Newton traveled to London for a Royal Society meeting. Two days later, he returned home very ill.

Newton had spent his entire life hiding his true religious feelings. But on his deathbed, he made one honest final gesture. He refused to take communion, a sacrament of the Church of England. He had searched for the truth of the universe his entire life. He said he felt no need to receive communion to prepare for his journey to another life. Sir Isaac Newton died on March 20, 1727.

Newton's body lay on display for a week, like a king's body would. Then he was buried with honor in Westminster Abbey. He was buried among kings and queens. On his monument was carved, "Let Mortals rejoice that there has existed so great an ornament to the Human Race."

Epilogue

Isaac Newton changed the world. When he was born, people saw the natural world as a mystery. Through his studies and relentless experiments, he discovered laws that helped people understand the natural world.

His legacy surrounds us. Microscopes, eyeglasses, and cameras are based on his discoveries about light and optics. And the largest telescopes are still reflecting telescopes. The Hale telescope at the Palomar Observatory in California is a large version of Newton's telescope. The Hale telescope uses a mirror that is two hundred inches in diameter.

Newton's laws of motion form the basis of mechanical engineering. Scientists in many fields rely on those laws. Engineers use them to design cars and roller coasters. They use them to build airplane engines. They rely on them to design steamships and suspension bridges. Many scientists still consider *The Principia* to be the most important scientific work ever published. Newton's discoveries are so central to the study of motion that the international unit of force is called a newton.

Newton did get some things wrong. He came up with incorrect ideas about the tides and the speed of sound. Even his famous law of universal gravitation isn't always true for extremely large or extremely tiny objects. Several centuries passed before another great scientist, Albert Einstein, explained why. Einstein respected Newton's genius. He said, "Nature to him was an open book, whose letters he could read without effort."

Scholars believe that Newton probably did invent calculus first. But Leibniz probably invented calculus independently. Most people agree today that neither man stole the idea from the other.

Neither Newton nor Hooke was completely correct about light. Newton believed light was composed of particles, while Hooke believed light was composed of waves. In his quantum theory of light, Einstein revealed that light travels as little bundles of energy. These bundles have characteristics of both waves and particles, although they are not entirely either one.

Still, Newton made astounding advances in his lifetime. He gave us many scientific methods. He used questions, practical experiments, and logic to answer questions about nature. He gave shape to the Scientific Revolution and revealed some of the elegant workings of nature. Yet he never lost sight of mysteries still unsolved. He never thought he had all the answers.

In his later years, Newton wrote, "I don't know what I may seem to the world, but, as to myself, I seem to have been only like a boy playing on the sea shore, and diverting myself in now and then finding a smoother pebble or a prettier shell than ordinary whilst the great ocean of truth lay all undiscovered before me."

Clearly, Newton did not remain on the seashore. He dove deep into the ocean of knowledge, and eventually he revealed its treasures to the world. A couplet by eighteenth-century poet Alexander Pope was engraved in the room at Woolsthorpe Manor where Newton was born:

> Nature and Nature's Laws lay hid in Night.
> God said, Let Newton be! and all was Light.

Newton's Major Discoveries

Calculus
This mathematical system lets the user figure out problems involving changes in speed, curved lines, and so on. Calculus has endless uses, such as planning the course of a spaceship.

Light
Newton discovered that white light was made up of all the colors of the spectrum. He was the first person to understand the composition of the rainbow. His work with light allowed scientists to learn about stars based on the light emitted by those stars.

Newton's laws of motion
1. *Law of inertia:* A body at rest tends to remain at rest, and a body in motion tends to remain in motion.
2. *Law of acceleration:* The acceleration of an object depends on the object's mass and the force that is applied to it.
3. *Law of action and reaction:* For every action, there is an equal and opposite reaction.

These fundamental laws of motion have dictated the development of everything from steamships to cars to airplane engines. The standard international unit of force is called the Newton.

Newton's law of universal gravitation
The force of gravity between any two bodies depends on their masses and their distance from each other. Newton used this law to prove that gravity was the force keeping planets in their orbits and apples falling toward the ground. This law allows scientists to predict the path of the planets.

Reflecting telescope
Newton made a new kind of telescope by reflecting light from a curved mirror rather than passing it through a curved lens. (A telescope that uses only lenses is called a refracting telescope.) This allowed perfect focus to be achieved for the first time, so scientists could study the skies much more accurately.

Selected Bibliography

Books and Articles

Andrade, Edward Neville da Costa. *Sir Isaac Newton: His Life and Work.* Garden City, NY: Doubleday & Company, 1954.

Berlinski, David. *Newton's Gift: How Sir Isaac Newton Unlocked the System of the World.* New York: Free Press, 2000.

Broad, William J. "Sir Isaac Newton: Mad as a Hatter," *Science,* September 18, 1981, pp. 1341– .

Carrell, Jennifer Lee. "Newton's Vice: Some Say Alchemy Inspired Our Greatest Scientist," *Smithsonian,* December 2000, pp. 130– .

Craig, John Herbert. *Newton at the Mint.* Cambridge, UK: Cambridge University Press, 1946.

De Morgan, Augustus. *Newton: His Friend and His Niece.* London: Elliot Stock, 1885.

Hall, A. Rupert. *Isaac Newton: Adventurer in Thought.* Cambridge, UK: Blackwell Publishers, 1992.

Harrison, John R. *The Library of Isaac Newton.* London: Cambridge University Press, 1978.

Hershman, D. Jablow, and Julian Lieb. *The Key to Genius: Manic-Depression and the Creative Life.* Buffalo, NY: Prometheus Books, 1988.

Manuel, Frank E. *A Portrait of Isaac Newton.* New York: Da Capo Press, 1968.

Newton, Sir Isaac. *Correspondence.* Edited by H. W. Turnbull. Cambridge, UK: Cambridge University Press, 1959.

Olsen, Kirstin. *Daily Life in 18th-Century England.* Westport, CT: Greenwood Press, 1999.

Strathern, Paul. *Newton and Gravity.* New York: Anchor Books, 1997.

Stukeley, William. *Memoirs of Sir Isaac Newton's Life.* London: Taylor and Francis, 1936.

Sullivant, Rosemary. "When the Apple Falls," *Astronomy,* April 1998, pp. 54– .

Westfall, Richard S. *The Life of Isaac Newton.* New York: Cambridge University Press, 1993.

Westfall, Richard S. *Never at Rest.* New York: Cambridge University Press, 1980.

Videos

Newton: *A Tale of Two Isaacs.* Steeplechase Entertainment, 1999. Videocassette.

Newton's Wagon: Understanding Motion. TMW Media Group, 2000. Videocassette.

Websites

Isaac Newton's Laws of Motion
<http://id.mind.net/~zona/mstm/physics/mechanics/forces/newton/newton.html>

Sir Isaac Newton and the Unification of Physics and Astronomy
<http://csep10.phys.utk.edu/astr161/lect/history/newton.html>

Index

alchemy, 37, 48, 53
Aristotle, 17–19
Ayscough, Hannah (mother), 6, 8, 12–13, 15–16, 39

Barrow, Isaac, 20, 33–34, 36
Barton, Catherine (niece), 51, 54–56

Calculus, 24, 37–38, 53, 54, 58, 60
Cambridge University, 16–18, 19–22, 33, 38–39, 46, 50; degrees from, 22, 33
Church of England, 38–39, 56
Clark, Mr., 8, 10, 15
colors, 28–30, 33
Conduitt, John, 54
Copernicus, Nicolaus, 19

"De Analysi," 33
Descartes, René, 19, 25

Einstein, Albert, 58

Galilei, Galileo, 18, 19
Grantham, England, 5, 8, 12, 15
gravity, 27–28, 32, 41, 44, 46

Halley, Edmund, 36, 40, 43, 54
Hooke, Robert, 36–37, 39, 41, 42, 46–47, 53, 58
Huygens, Christiaan, 31

inverse square law of gravity, 27, 39, 41, 42, 46

Kepler, Johannes, 19, 24
King's School, 8, 15, 16

law of acceleration, 44, 60
law of action and reaction, 44, 60
law of inertia, 43, 60
laws of motion, 43–44, 58, 60
law of universal gravitation, 44, 58, 60
Leibniz, Gottfried, 37–38, 53, 54, 58
light, 28–30, 32, 34, 57, 58, 60
Locke, John, 36, 50
London, 50–51

mathematics, 19, 20, 30, 33–34, 39, 46. *See also* calculus
mechanics, 25, 32, 57
mills, 10–12
mint, the, 50–53, 54, 56

Newton, Sir Isaac: antisocial behavior, 8–9, 15, 48; birth, 5–6; childhood, 5–12; farming, 13–16; professor, 34, 46; religious beliefs, 19–20, 38–39, 47, 56

Oldenburg, Henry, 36

Opticks, 54
orbits, 24, 25–27, 41, 44

Parliament, 47, 50
Pepys, Samuel, 48–50
plague, the, 23–24, 30
Plato, 18
The Principia, 41–46, 53, 57
prism, 22, 28–30

Royal Society, 31, 36, 38, 42,
    46, 53–54, 56

Scientific Revolution, 17, 58
Smith, Benjamin (half brother),
    8, 39
Smith, Barnabas (stepfather),
    6, 8
Smith, Hannah (half sister), 8
Smith, Mary (half sister), 8
Storer, Arthur, 8–9
Storer, Edward, 8
Storer, Miss, 8, 12, 32
sundials, 10–11
System of the World, The, 44

telescopes, 19, 34–36, 57, 60
Tower of London, 51
Trinity College. *See* Cambridge
    University

universe, order in, 19, 46, 58

Woolsthorpe Manor, 5–8, 15,
    24–32, 39, 59